Color Me Bernie
Join The Bernie Coloring Revolution

by Leslie Tran

Color Me Bernie: Join The Bernie Coloring Revolution

ISBN-13: 9780692690925
ISBN-10: 692690921

Give feedback on the book at:
ColorMeBernie@gmail.com

Printed in U.S.A

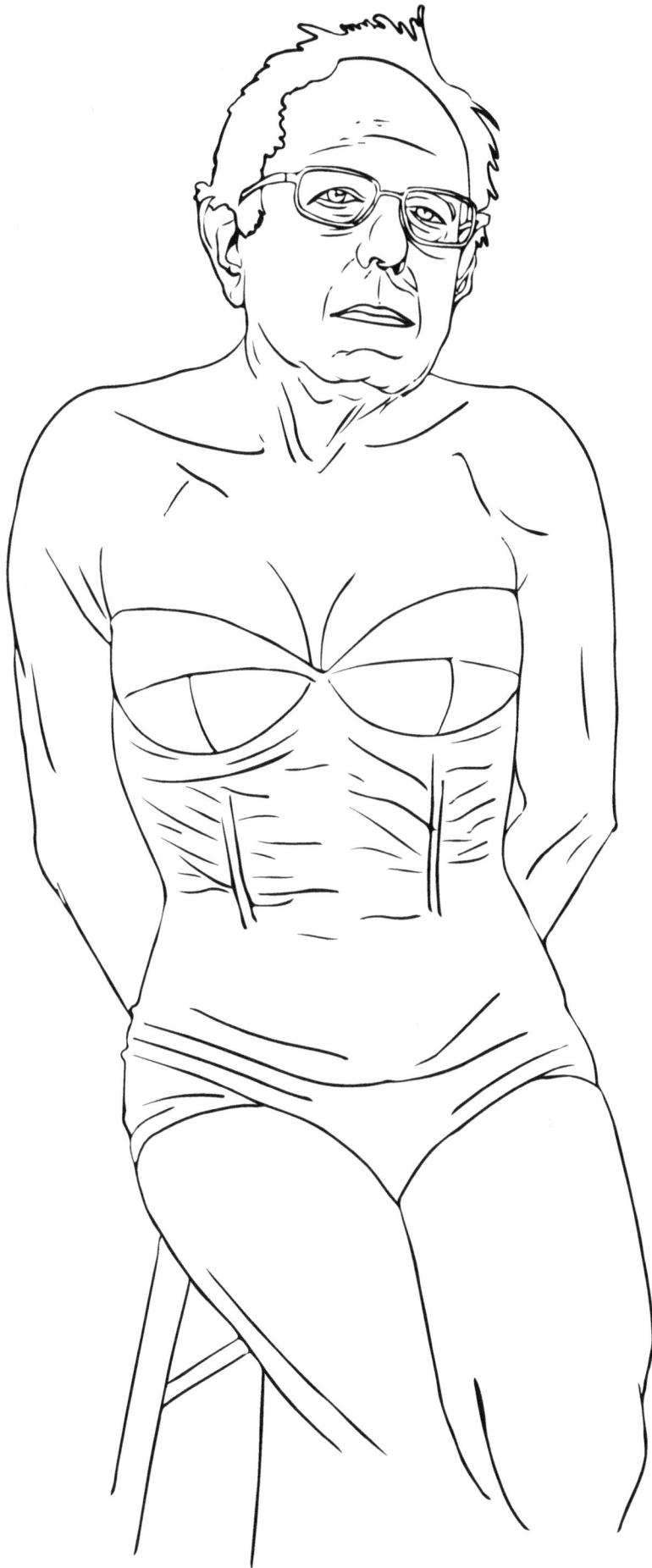

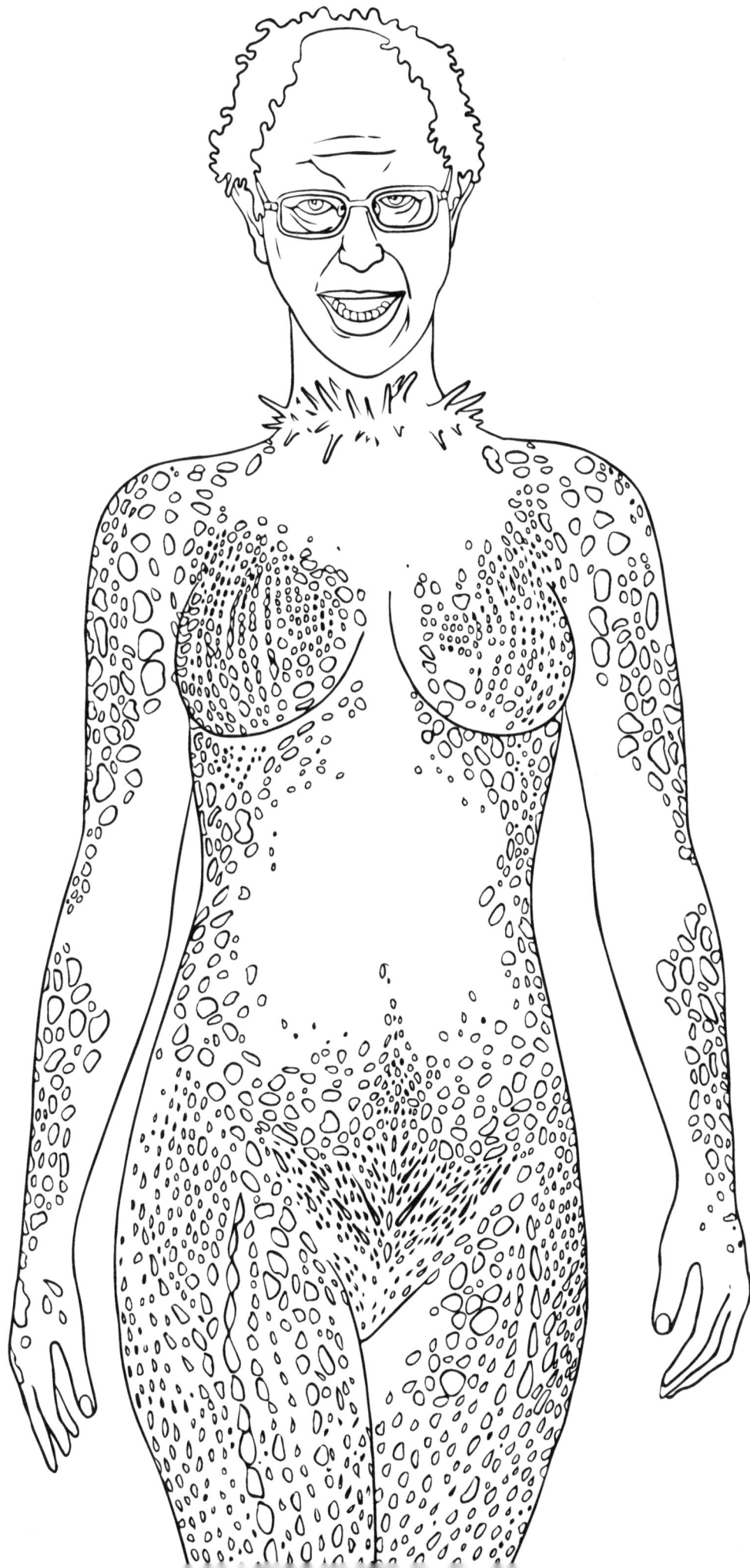

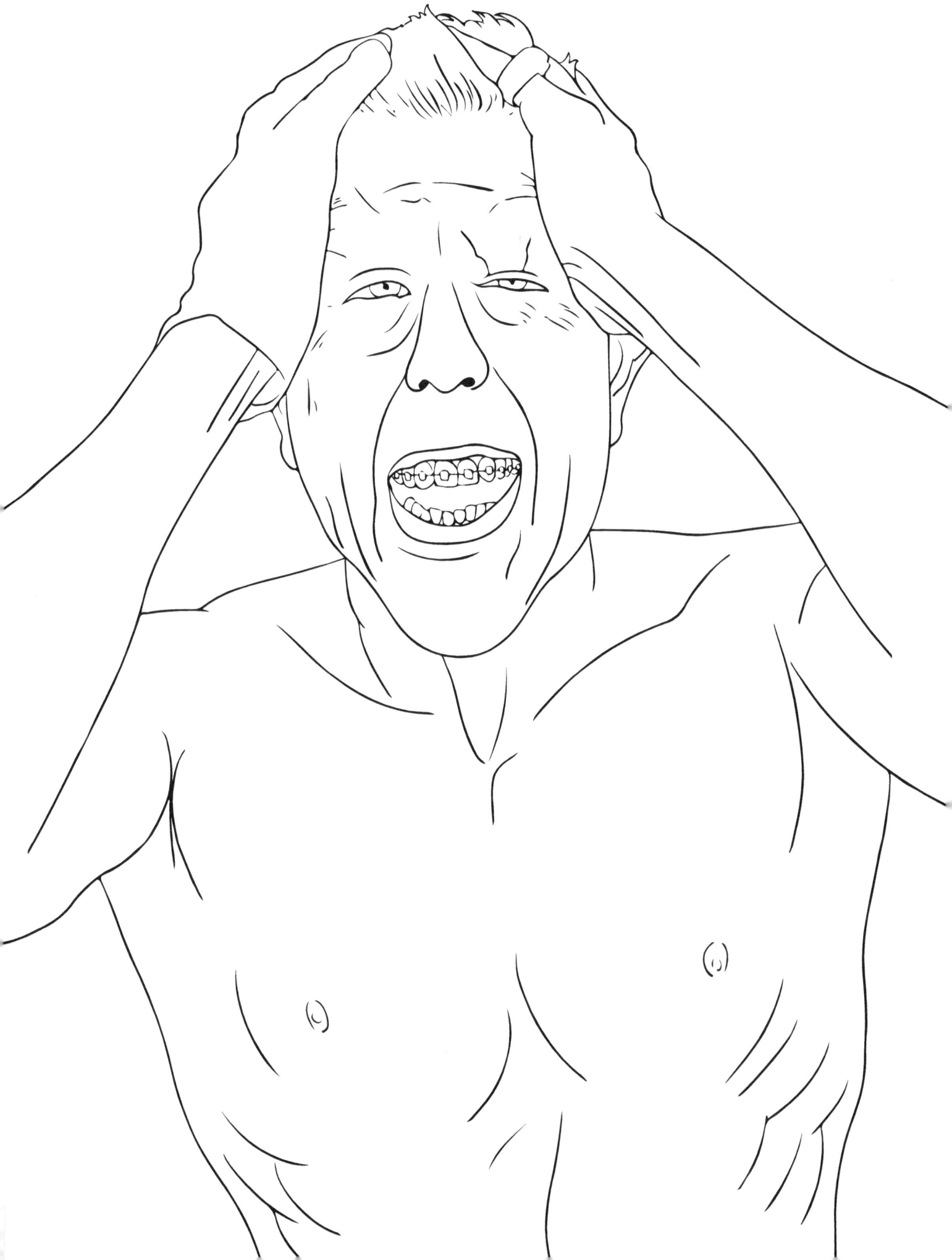

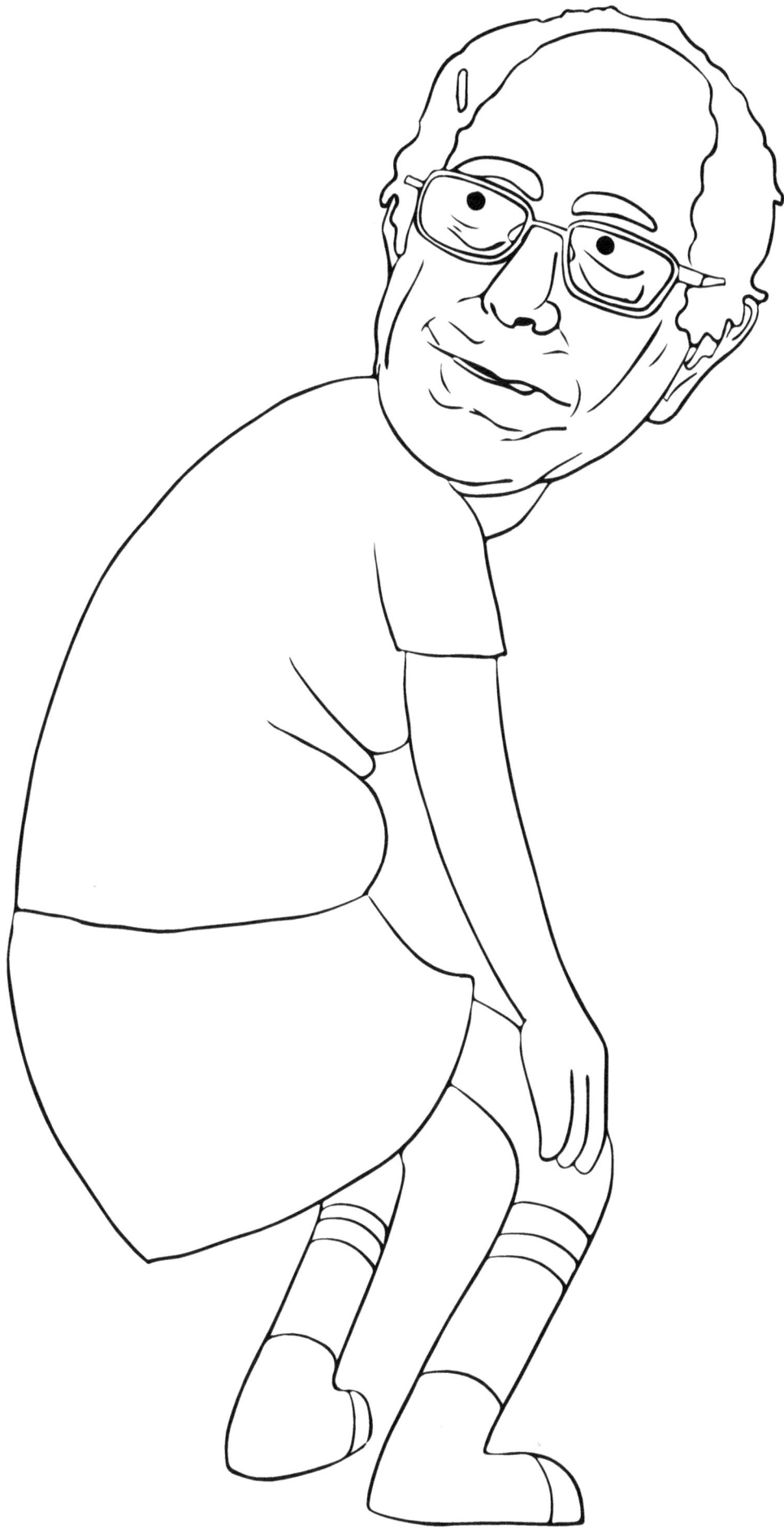

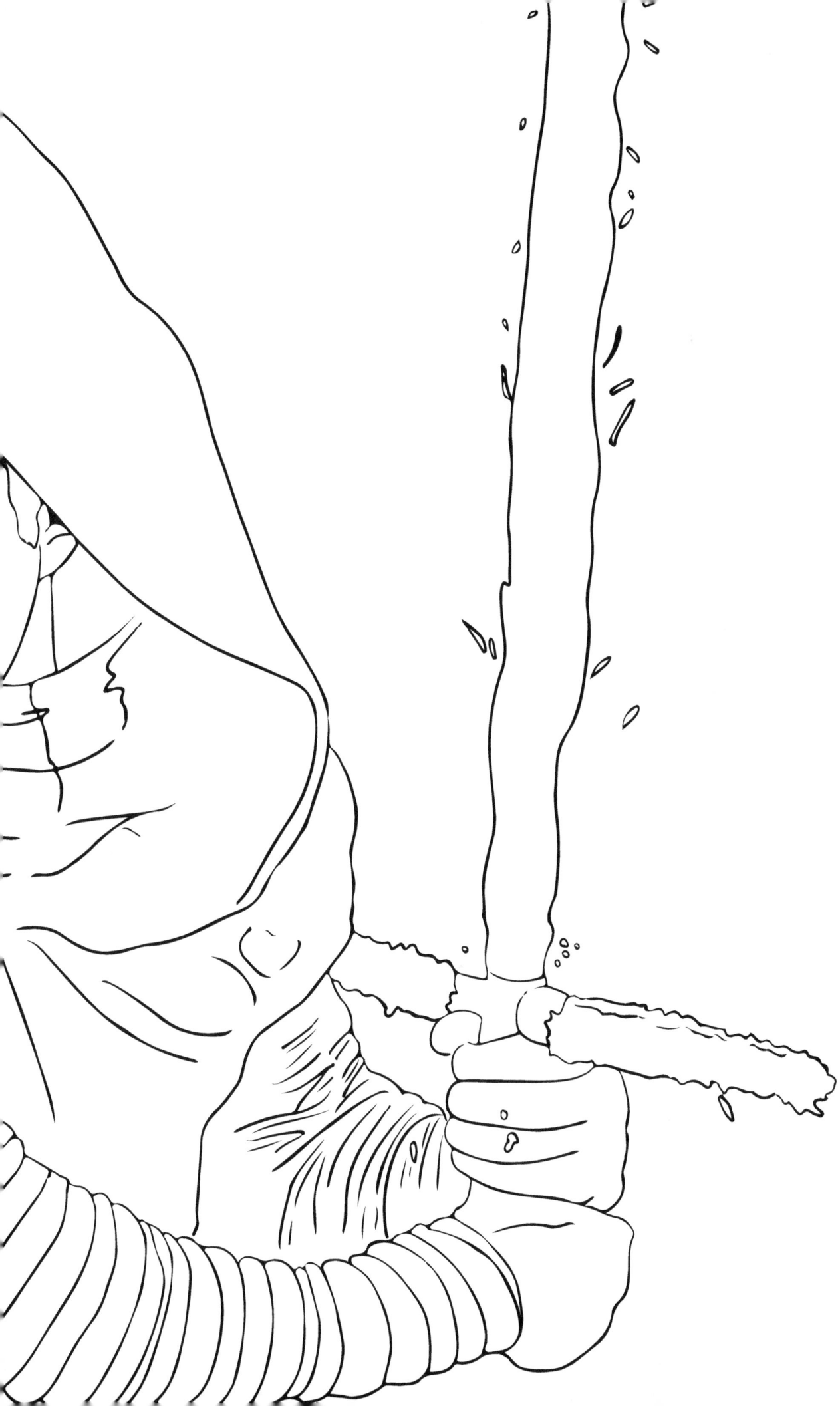

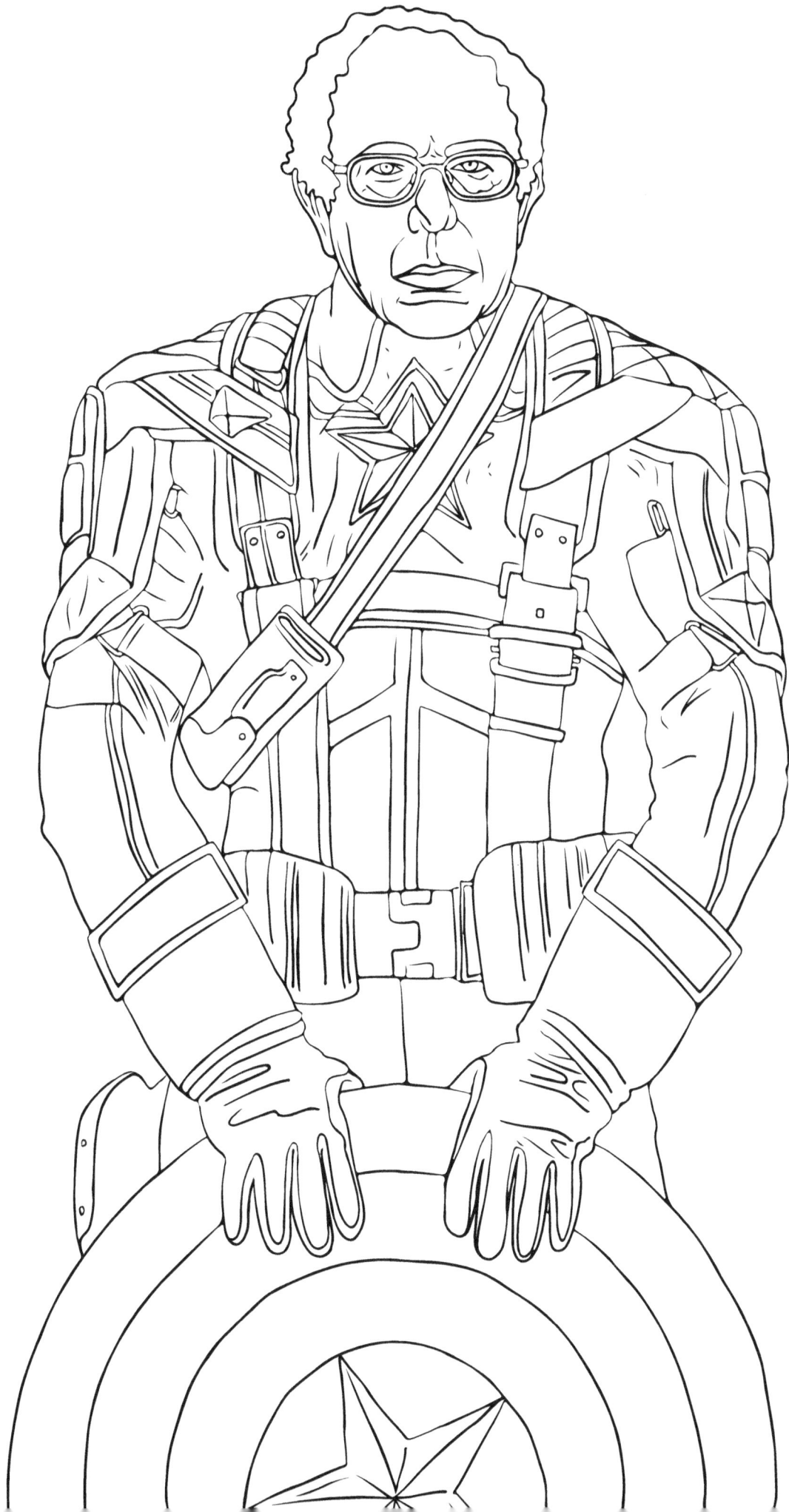